THE IDEAS INTO ACTION SERIES DRAWS ON THE
PRACTICAL KNOWLEDGE THAT THE CENTER FOR
CREATIVE LEADERSHIP (CCL®), SINCE ITS INCEPTION IN
1970, HAS GENERATED THROUGH ITS RESEARCH AND
EDUCATIONAL ACTIVITIES CONDUCTED IN PARTNERSHIP
WITH HUNDREDS OF THOUSANDS OF LEADERS. MUCH
OF THIS KNOWLEDGE IS SHARED—IN A WAY THAT IS
DISTINCT FROM THE TYPICAL UNIVERSITY DEPARTMENT,
PROFESSIONAL ASSOCIATION, OR CONSULTANCY. CCL
IS NOT SIMPLY A COLLECTION OF INDIVIDUAL EXPERTS,
ALTHOUGH THE INDIVIDUAL CREDENTIALS OF ITS
STAFF ARE IMPRESSIVE; RATHER IT IS A COMMUNITY,
WITH ITS MEMBERS HOLDING CERTAIN PRINCIPLES IN
COMMON AND WORKING TOGETHER TO UNDERSTAND
AND GENERATE PRACTICAL RESPONSES TO TODAY'S
LEADERSHIP AND ORGANIZATIONAL CHALLENGES.
THE PURPOSE OF THE SERIES IS TO PROVIDE LEADERS
WITH SPECIFIC ADVICE ON HOW TO COMPLETE A
DEVELOPMENTAL TASK OR SOLVE A LEADERSHIP
CHALLENGE. IN DOING THAT, THE SERIES CARRIES OUT
CCL'S MISSION TO ADVANCE THE UNDERSTANDING,
PRACTICE, AND DEVELOPMENT OF LEADERSHIP FOR THE
BENEFIT OF SOCIETY WORLDWIDE. WE THINK YOU WILL
FIND THE IDEAS INTO ACTION SERIES AN IMPORTANT
ADDITION TO YOUR LEADERSHIP TOOLKIT.

CATHLEEN CLERKIN, PHD., IS THE SENIOR DIRECTOR
OF RESEARCH AT CANDID. AT THE TIME OF WRITING
THIS BOOK, SHE WAS THE MANAGER OF STRATEGIC
RESEARCH AND A SENIOR RESEARCH SCIENTIST AT THE
CENTER FOR CREATIVE LEADERSHIP. HER RESEARCH
INTERESTS INCLUDE ISSUES OF EQUITY, DIVERSITY
AND INCLUSION, SOCIAL IDENTITY, INNOVATION, AND
HOLISTIC APPROACHES TO LEADERSHIP DEVELOPMENT.
CATHLEEN HAS A PHD IN PSYCHOLOGY FROM THE
UNIVERSITY OF MICHIGAN, AND A B.A. FROM UC
BERKELEY.

SPECIAL THANKS TO JESSICA DAVIDSON, VALERIE
EHRLICH, AND BROOK WINGATE FOR REVIEWING AN
EARLY VERSION OF THIS WORK.

Beyond Bias™

Move from Awareness to Action

Cathleen Clerkin

978-1-64761-000-5 – PRINT

978-1-64761-001-2 – EBOOK

CCL NO 474

**PUBLISHED BY THE CENTER FOR CREATIVE LEADERSHIP
CCL PRESS**

AUTHOR: CATHLEEN CLERKIN

EDITOR: SHAUN MARTIN

RIGHTS AND PERMISSIONS: WWW.CCL.ORG/PERMISSION-
REPUBLISH-REQUEST/

DESIGN AND LAYOUT: SARA ANN HOWARD

CONTENTS

WHAT IS BIAS?

Ben Barres was an American neurobiologist at Stanford University, known for his research on glial cells in the nervous system. According to *The Wall Street Journal*, he gave a seminar in the late 1990s on some of his latest research to a prestigious group of top scientists. The presentation was well-received. Afterward, a friend told him one of the scientists commented how impressive the seminar was and how "Ben Barres' work is much better than his sister's."[1] The problem is, Ben didn't have a sister who did scientific work. Ben was a transgender man who had recently transitioned. In fact, the very research he had presented was conducted while he was known as Barbara.

Ben's experience is an example of gender bias. Bias, broadly defined, **is an intentional or unintentional preference for or against a specific group or individual**. In this case, there was a bias towards seeing men as brilliant scientists, resulting in the audience member being more impressed by Ben's research when he appeared masculine. A plethora of research confirms that gender bias is a widely experienced issue across many organizations and industries, and testimonies from transgender individuals who have experienced both the **for** and the **against** aspects of gender bias certainly make it hard to deny.

Bias can occur in almost any situation that includes making a judgment about something or someone, and is especially likely to happen when there are differing perspectives, experiences, and social groups. For instance, racial bias is common, with certain racial groups intentionally or unintentionally preferred over others. Such preferences often lead to differences in treatment and evaluation. Notable examples of the dire consequences that

Imagine your organization brought in a diverse group of possible candidates for a directorship position. There are individuals who are: men, women, non-binary, tall, short, tattooed, gray haired, pink haired, young, old, obese, dark-skinned, light-skinned, disabled, shy, and outgoing. How might you and others in your organization react to these candidates? Who would fit in? Who would stand out? Who would people trust in this leadership role? Who would people be hesitant about? Who would people be afraid of? Who would people feel pity towards?

Most of us would like to say these attributes would not play a role in the candidate selection process. However, more often than not, cultural assumptions and biases around some of these attributes do in fact impact how we perceive leadership ability and potential.

can result from racial bias are the killing of George Floyd and other Black Americans at the hands of the U.S. police. These actions suggest a bias towards perceiving Black Americans as more aggressive and dangerous, and/or more acceptable to be aggressive towards, which in turn can result in discrimination, violence, and ultimately murder.

Bias in the workplace in particular often happens when specific employees and/or leaders do not fit social expectations. While the specific standards might vary by country and culture, every society has implicit norms—and implicit bias—around what identities, characteristics, and physical attributes are desirable and preferred. It is common to have biases around nationality, age, physical appearance (e.g. height, weight, hairstyles), disabilities, culture, religion, and sexual orientation, in addition to gender and race. Most of us are uncomfortable with the idea of bias. We want to treat people fairly and want to believe that others have fair and equal treatment and opportunities. This can lead us to believing that we are not biased, or that bias is not common. Unfortunately, research suggests this is not the case. Rather, bias is part of the human condition. Moving hurriedly in a complex world, we are easily overwhelmed and distracted. Our brains help us navigate this complexity by making quick and automatic decisions, shortcuts, and assumptions in order to minimize the amount of energy it takes us to function. In many cases, such shortcuts are helpful and important for expediency and effectiveness (imagine how exhausting it would be if we had to actively remember to breathe, or if we did not have mental shortcuts telling us which objects to sit on when we entered a new room).

However, these shortcuts can also backfire and lead us to faulty conclusions and biases. For example, inaccurate guesses about who will make the best leader, or who is likely to do us harm. This happens to every single one of us regardless of our intelligence, intentions, or values. And, unfortunately, when it happens we usually don't even realize it. Because of this, it is essential to recognize that bias plays a critical role in defining our reality. While you may feel like your experience and interpretation of events is objective and complete, your brain is constantly making assumptions, associations, and jumping to conclusions that you might not even notice. We are especially likely to fall prone to biases when we are stressed, tired, or distracted. During such times, our brains are worn down, and so we are more likely to rely on assumptions or shortcuts **and** less likely to notice when we are doing so.

REFLECTION

Have you never noticed yourself making assumptions about others when you were stressed, distracted, upset, or low on sleep?

Why Addressing Bias is Essential for Leaders

Understanding and working toward eliminating bias is an admirable goal for anyone, but it is vital for leaders in particular. Leaders make decisions that change lives. They decide who is hired, promoted, or dismissed; where to invest funds, when to bet on new ideas, and what the future of their organizations will be. Because bias can shape assumptions about what certain people can do—often leading to inaccurate evaluations of both performance and potential—leaders who address bias are better able to fully leverage their teams.

Mitigating the effects of bias can also increase leaders' ability to notice new trends, calculate risk, and read situations. This is because bias essentially relies on assumptions and over-generalizations. Such short-cuts often fail to recognize the full complexity of a given situation, leading to errors and faulty logic. Perhaps most importantly, unchecked bias among leaders

UNDERSTANDING AND WORKING TOWARD
ELIMINATING BIAS IS AN ADMIRABLE GOAL
FOR ANYONE, BUT IT IS VITAL FOR LEADERS IN
PARTICULAR. LEADERS MAKE DECISIONS THAT
CHANGE LIVES. THEY DECIDE WHO IS HIRED,
PROMOTED, OR DISMISSED; WHERE TO INVEST
FUNDS, WHEN TO BET ON NEW IDEAS, AND WHAT
THE FUTURE OF THEIR ORGANIZATIONS WILL BE.

can ripple through organizations, resulting in a climate where employees feel excluded, unvalued, and unsafe. In contrast, leaders who are savvy at noticing and addressing bias are more likely to be seen as inclusive leaders who are prepared to lead diverse groups.

While bias has always been an issue relevant to leadership, the connection has become hard to ignore in recent years. The quickly escalating globalization and diversification of the workforce, coupled with the increased social demand for justice, equity, diversity, and inclusion, has made understanding bias critical for anyone with leadership aspirations or responsibilities. This book will help leaders better understand what bias is, how you can recognize it, and what you can do about it.

TYPES OF BIAS

The word bias is tossed around a lot and is often used to mean many different things. Some scholars have argued the word "bias" has become so overused that it's all but lost its meaning. For you to understand how to do something about bias in your life, it's helpful first to explore how bias works and the different ways it can occur.

Theorists believe the word "bias" was first used in English in the 1600s as a technical term in the British game of bowls to describe a particular type of ball that was purposefully weighted on one side. These "biased" balls did not roll in a straight line but somewhat curved as they rolled. This serves as an excellent analogy for understanding bias today. A ball with an uneven distribution of weight might appear to be balanced at first glance, but it doesn't play out that way. Instead, it has a hidden yet consistent preference for one side over another, making it challenging to aim true. But, over time and with practice, *if you know the bias is there, you can learn to course correct*.

Inspired by this concept, legal and statistical professions soon began using the word bias to describe circumstances that were not fair or accurate, but rather distorted or prejudiced, or "causing to incline to one side."[2] Soon, the term spread to social sciences, where the modern definition comes from: an intentional or unintentional preference for or against a specific group or individual.

In particular, scientists have heavily researched two types of psychological bias: cognitive bias and implicit associations. Typically, when people talk about bias, they are referring to one of these phenomena.

COGNITIVE BIAS

"Cognitive bias" refers to common mental shortcuts that are not entirely logical and rational. These mental tendencies are often a result of early socio-cultural learning or evolutionary preferences. Here are some examples of common cognitive biases:

Name of Bias	Definition
Correspondence Bias	The tendency to assume that a person's behaviors reflect their permanent disposition or personality, when such behaviors could actually be entirely explained by the situation.
Confirmation Bias	The tendency to listen to and focus on information that confirms previously held beliefs.

Name of Bias	Definition
Hindsight Bias	The tendency to see events, even random ones, as predictable, leading to us looking back and believing that we "knew it all along."
Self-serving Bias	The tendency to give ourselves credit for successes but blame failures on causes outside ourselves or our control.
Outcome Bias	The tendency to evaluate decisions based on their outcomes, not based on how the decision was made.
In-group Bias	The tendency to favor others who belong to our own social group(s).
Affinity Bias	The tendency to like others who are like ourselves.
Status Quo Bias	The tendency to prefer the current state of affairs.
Blind-spot Bias	The tendency not to notice our own biases.

There are hundreds of cognitive biases, but these examples highlight the point: we make mental shortcuts all the time, often without realizing it, and thoughts or decisions we feel are logical and objective may be more biased and subjective than we realize.

REFLECTION

In looking at these nine common cognitive biases, can you think of a time when you might have fallen prey to these faulty ways of thinking? What was going on at the time? Were there specific circumstances that made you more prone to these biases?

How might these biases impact your ability to lead effectively? Does your organization tend to rely on any of these biases? If so, how have they impacted organizational culture, decision making, or performance?

IMPLICIT ASSOCIATIONS

Another category of psychological bias is implicit associations. Implicit associations occur when our brains make connections between otherwise unassociated concepts (this is also sometimes called "implicit bias," "implicit stereotypes," or "implicit social cognition").[3] For example, in a classic study, researchers asked students to "draw a scientist" without giving them any further instructions. The most common image drawn was one of a man in a lab coat wearing glasses.[4] This finding suggests that there is an implicit association between being a "scientist" and being a "man," "wearing glasses," and "wearing a lab coat". Implicit associations are often made between certain groups or identities and their behaviors or abilities. However, implicit associations can also apply to other ideas or concepts as well.

A fundamental tenet of implicit associations is that we do not necessarily make these associations intentionally. Rather, implicit associations simply describe what associations are 'wired' into our brains through cultural norms. Indeed, many implicit association studies have found that people may explicitly state one belief (e.g., that all genders are equally good at science or that all races are equally smart) but that their implicit association scores reveal other associations they might not necessarily condone.

There has been some debate as to what this discrepancy suggests. For example, some have argued that implicit associations reveal the "truth" as to whether people are racist, sexist, etc. Others have argued that implicit associations are faulty measures because they don't always align with the beliefs people explicitly endorse. However, leaders in the field urge us not to jump to either of these conclusions. Rather, implicit associations are just what they claim to be: a measure of the extent to which our brain associates different concepts. This doesn't necessarily reflect our morals or explicit beliefs, but merely how our brains have connected pieces of information it has encountered out in the world. As such, it is a better measure of social and cultural norms than personal values. At the same time, implicit bias can play a role in how we treat people and process information, so understanding and acknowledging our implicit associations can help us determine what we need to do to make sure that our impact match our intentions.

TEST YOUR IMPLICIT ASSOCIATIONS

Many free online tools offer you the opportunity to explore your implicit associations. For example, try Harvard University's ongoing Project Implicit https://implicit.harvard.edu/implicit/takeatest.html. This project allows you to select which common associations you want to test, automatically and confidentially scores your associations, and shows you whether your associations are stronger or weaker than average.

IS BIAS UNCONSCIOUS?

There has been a lot of debate lately about whether bias is "conscious" or "unconscious." The answer is: it's complicated. Indeed, people often have implicit associations they do not explicitly endorse. However, this does not necessarily mean the associations happen "unconsciously." Perhaps a better description is that they are "unintentional" or "autopilot" responses. Much like you can drive a car "on autopilot" and get to your destination without quite realizing how you got there, you can also have associations and make assumptions without quite realizing you are doing so.

And of course, not all bias is unintentional. There are plenty of cases where bias is deliberate and explicit. For example, when people explicitly endorse negative stereotypes or actively promote oppression or hate speech towards a group of people, these are forms of intentional and explicit bias. As a leader, it is important to realize that intentional bias still happens every day, and assuming that all bias is unintended or unconscious can be a disservice if you are trying to help those who may be the target of bias. To complicate things even further, it is often hard to know how intentional or unintentional bias is in real-life situations. For example, in the case of Ben at the beginning of this book, it is unclear whether the audience member specifically endorsed Ben's abilities because he was a man, or whether they didn't realize how gender was influencing their perceptions.

BIAS IS A HABIT

Because bias is nebulous, pervasive, and often unintended, it is easy to think that there isn't much that you can do about it. This, in turn, can feel frustrating and overwhelming. However, recent research suggests there are several things that you can do to decrease bias in—and out of—the workplace. Ideas, tips, and suggestions on how to take action to address bias are included throughout this book and highlighted in the SCRIPt™ toolkit in the last section.

A vital step in taking action against bias is recognizing that bias can be categorized as a **habit**. This might seem odd at first, but world-renowned bias researcher Dr. Patricia Devine at the University of Wisconsin suggests that bias is exactly that: a habit. One definition of a habit is "a more or less fixed way of thinking, willing, or feeling acquired through previous repetition of a mental experience."[5] Once we get in the routine of doing something, it then happens with very little thought or effort; it becomes a habit. One reason that habits are so hard to break is because neurons that fire together wire together. When you do something repetitively, your brain reinforces that particular pathway. Over time, they can become our default, "auto-pilot" reactions. This is true of bias as well: bias is a result of routinized attitudes, beliefs, associations, and shortcuts that have been learned and reinforced throughout our lives.

Realizing that bias is a habit can help us understand how to do something about it. Chances are you've developed a bad habit at some point in your life, and chances are, you've also tried breaking it. If so, you know that breaking habits takes hard work, but it is also possible. With enough practice, we can break old habits and wire our brains for new ones. Our habit of bias is no different. Changing a habit requires awareness, motivation, confidence, and deliberate, regular practice of new thoughts or behaviors to replace the old ones.

REFLECTION

What is a bad habit that you've successfully broken? What did it take for you to finally break the habit? What can you take from your previous experience breaking habits to help you challenge the habit of bias?

2

The Beyond Bias Model

A second important step in mitigating the effects of bias is better understanding how bias can transform from a mental shortcut or association into real life challenges in the workplace.

Beyond Bias™ Model

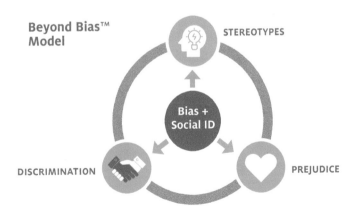

STEREOTYPES

Bias + Social ID

DISCRIMINATION

PREJUDICE

The Beyond Bias Model helps demonstrate how bias goes beyond your brain, resulting in stereotypes, prejudice, and discrimination. The Beyond Bias model offers a simplified snapshot of how bias can lead to stereotypes, prejudice, and discrimination. A critical factor in this transformation has to do with social identity. While the abstract concept of "bias" as a preference can be mundane (e.g., people may profess a bias against romantic comedies or towards spicy food), it becomes detrimental when it is aimed towards specific identities or group of people (e.g. gender bias, racial bias), as highlighted at the beginning of this book. It is the intersection and combination of these two elements that then becomes the crucible and catalyst for workplace problems; and are thus in the center of the model.

The outer ring of the model highlights the three outcomes you are likely to see in the workplace (or elsewhere) when bias interacts with social identity: stereotypes, prejudice, and discrimination. One way to remember the three outcomes of this model is to think about the analogy of "Head, Heart, and Hands": Stereotyping is about beliefs (Head), prejudice is about emotions (Heart), and discrimination is about actions (Hands). You will notice that there are no arrows showing causality between the three outcomes because they are all equally and closely connected—each often increases another, but not in a particular, causal order. In the next sections, we dive deeper into each part of this model.

SOCIAL IDENTITY

Social identities are the parts of your identity derived from group membership. Common social identities include gender, race, culture, religion, generation, nationality, (dis)ability, political affiliation, profession, and many others. We all have multiple social identities, and the combination of identities often influences how we see the world and how others treat us. We also all have our own unique experiences of our identities. Some identities might seem important, others more superficial. Some identities might be stable; others may change over time. We might be very open about some of our identities, while others we might consider very private. Finding others who share your social identities can offer a sense of belonging and validation. Social identities can also create motivation and action. We may feel called to mobilize, speak out, or organize based on a social identity.

However, social identities and social groups can also trigger bias. For example, a well-established cognitive bias is in-group bias: the bias towards preferring those from our in-groups (e.g., those who share our social identities). Social identities can also activate affinity bias, our tendency to like others who are like ourselves. We view our ingroups and people who seem similar to us more favorably and view their words and actions in a more charitable light. Psychologically, we have a strong motivation for favoring others like us and our groups, as doing so boosts our

REFLECTION

Think about your own social identities. How might these identities impact how you view your team? Your organization? What assumptions might you be making because of your specific lived experiences? What assumptions might others be making about you and your leadership because of your identities? What do you know about the social identities of your team members? What assumptions might you be making about them and their identities?

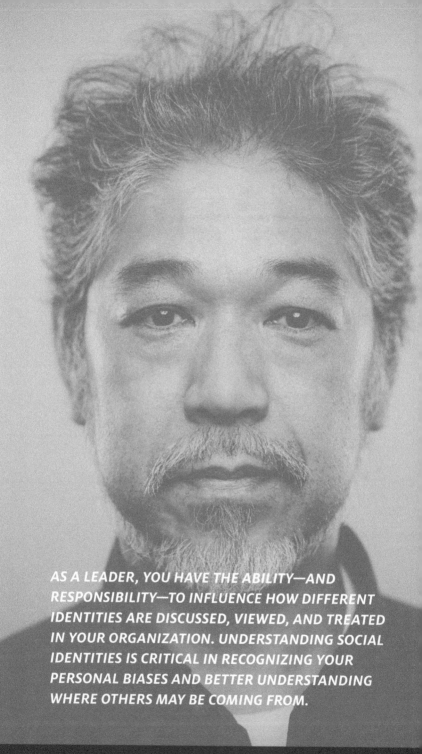

AS A LEADER, YOU HAVE THE ABILITY—AND RESPONSIBILITY—TO INFLUENCE HOW DIFFERENT IDENTITIES ARE DISCUSSED, VIEWED, AND TREATED IN YOUR ORGANIZATION. UNDERSTANDING SOCIAL IDENTITIES IS CRITICAL IN RECOGNIZING YOUR PERSONAL BIASES AND BETTER UNDERSTANDING WHERE OTHERS MAY BE COMING FROM.

self-esteem, making us proud of who we are and the groups we belong to. Of course, the downside of this is that we tend to treat people different from us more harshly—whether or not we realize it—requiring them to work harder to gain our approval and trust. Therefore, the combination of bias and social identity groups can spark stereotypes, prejudice, and discrimination.

We also tend to have implicit associations about different social identity groups—and often we aren't even aware of these associations or preferences. As a leader, you have the ability—and responsibility—to influence how different identities are discussed, viewed, and treated in your organization. Understanding social identities is critical in recognizing your personal biases and better understanding where others may be coming from. The more you are aware of your social identities, the social identities of others, and the factors that influence their ability to express these identities, the more you can work towards creating a workplace and society that recognizes, respects, celebrates, and includes diverse people.

STEREOTYPES

Stereotypes are generalized beliefs about social identity groups and their members. For example, we may believe that certain ethnic groups are lazy, strong, or ugly; or that certain genders are emotional, tough, or smart; or that certain generations are entitled, hardworking, or virtuous. Stereotypes can feel true because society has reinforced these associations through repetition. However, such simplistic generalizations are never true of every person within a given group, and perpetuating stereotypes can cause a surprising amount of harm.

For example, a study conducted by the University of Michigan demonstrated that Black women's awareness of others holding negative stereotypes of their group had detrimental consequences for their own health and well-being, including increased depression and anxiety and diminished self-care.[6] In other words, simply knowing that others have stereotypes about you can make it harder for you to perform at your best.

Stereotypes can also be a self-fulfilling prophesy that impacts performance. For example, one study found that when Asian American women were reminded about their gender right before a math test, their performance went down (fulfilling the stereotype that women are bad at math). In contrast, when they were reminded about their race, performance went up (fulfilling the stereotype that Asians are good at math).[7] This phenomenon is sometimes referred to as **stereotype threat**, because the mere existence of stereotypes can pose a threat to performance. In short, stereotypes in the workplace can create an invisible burden on those targeted, impacting both work performance and well-being.

REFLECTION

1. Most of us have been stereotyped at some point in our lives. Can you think of a time when someone interacted with you in a way that suggested they held a stereotype about one of your social identities? What did they say or do? How did it feel? What did you think? What did you do?

2. While we might like to think that stereotypes don't happen anymore in the workplace, research suggests they are still very common. How might stereotypes impact members of your team? How might stereotypes influence who gets hired and promoted in your workplace? What can you do to prevent stereotypes from doing harm?

PREJUDICE

The second potential consequence of the intersection of bias and social identities is prejudice. Prejudice is unfavorable emotional or affective reactions toward a group and its members. Psychologists believe that prejudice happens because we are naturally protective of our in-groups, and "outsiders" can feel threatening. Because of this, prejudice is more likely to occur when there is a perceived threat to the goals or welfare of your in-groups. People often assume that outsiders will block the in-group's shared goals either by directly competing or by simply having different goals. Interrupted goals can create anger, frustration, anxiety, disgust, discomfort, and fear—all emotions commonly directed toward outgroups. These emotions may be expressed externally or bubble below the surface, perhaps not even being internally acknowledged.

Prejudice is often sparked as a reaction to a novel situation or a change or disruption. For example, encountering someone from a foreign culture or who has a different worldview or value set than you do. Similarly, the blending of two previously separate groups can also trigger feelings of threat and unease: because in such situations, we may not know the customs or ground rules for interaction. We may even feel reactive prejudice against groups or individuals we believe do not like or approve of us. On the other hand, familiarity tends to decrease prejudice as we are less likely to be threatened by individuals, groups, or circumstances that we are accustomed to.

While prejudice can be harder to notice than stereotypes, the impact is often more severe. In a meta-analysis of 23 studies, prejudice was a consistent, stronger predictor of discrimination than stereotypes.[8]

1. Have you ever experienced a time at work when your "in-group" felt threatened? Perhaps someone from another workgroup suggested that your team's funding should be cut. Or someone suggested that the political party that you align with should not be in power. Or that the clothing or hairstyles of one of your in-groups was not professional. What emotions did you feel? What goals were in conflict at that moment?

2. Prejudice research suggests that different emotions tend to be sparked in different situations.[9] Examine the chart on the following page and reflect on why you may have felt a certain way.

EMOTION	DEFINITIONS
Anger	Anger is often sparked when threat or harm to ourselves or our in-groups is ongoing and unjustified.
Fear	Fear is the most common emotional reaction when harm to ourselves or our in-groups seems likely or certain to happen in the near future.
Anxiety	Anxiety is felt when there is a potential harm or threat to ourselves or our in-group in the future, but it is uncertain whether it will happen.
Sadness	Sadness is most often felt when harm to ourselves or our in-group has happened in the past.

3. As a leader, what can you do to create common goals to decrease prejudice at work? What can you do to make your team feel psychologically safe in order to reduce feelings of threat?

DISCRIMINATION

The third potential negative consequence of bias related to social identity is discrimination. Discrimination is the differential treatment of certain groups and their members. In the workplace, this can include actions such as distributing unequitable jobs, salaries, assignments, benefits, or evaluations of people based on their group membership. There is a wealth of research and data demonstrating that discrimination happens in the workplace regularly, although it may not always be readily noticed or openly discussed.

For example, in a 2019 study, five thousand middle-aged U.S. workers were asked whether they felt discriminated against at their job because of their race, ethnic origin, sex/gender, age, or any other reason.[10] All social identity groups reported some level of discrimination, with Black women reporting experiencing the highest rates of discrimination (1 in 4) and white men reporting the lowest rates (1 in 10).

Other research suggests that these numbers are probably low. In a recent field study, ten young men of approximately the same age, appearance, verbal skills, and interaction styles were randomly given fake resumes with identical backgrounds and work experience and trained to behave in identical ways during interviews.[11] They then applied to the same 340 entry-level jobs in New York City. White men received callbacks or job offers in 31% of the jobs, compared to 25% of Latino applicants and just 15% of Black applicants. Because the researchers controlled the other typical qualification criteria, it appears that (implicit or explicit) racial discrimination (perhaps driven by racial stereotypes or prejudice) caused this difference in the overall distribution of who got hired.

Interestingly, however, the applicants largely did not feel they were being treated differently or unfairly at the time. It wasn't until they compared notes that the discrimination became apparent. For example, one retail clothing store told both the Black and

REFLECTION

As a leader, what steps have you taken to protect against discrimination in your team? What steps has your organization taken to examine whether discrimination is an issue in different levels and departments of the organization?

the Latino applicants that the position had been filled. However, the White applicant, who was interviewed after the other two, was offered the job on the spot. Similarly, another organization told both the Black and Latino candidates that they didn't qualify for consideration due to lack of job experience, while the White candidate was told that he didn't have the right job experience, but the organization would still set up a second interview.

These small differences, such as giving one person a chance over another, might not have felt significant to the interviewers. However, done repetitively and at scale, they can have a substantial impact on individuals' career opportunities and trajectories. In this way, a helpful analogy for understanding the consequences of bias is to think about rainwater. Single droplets seem delicate and harmless. But rain droplets landing in the same spot, again and again, can cause a considerable amount of damage, such as flooding or erosion. Similarly, our beliefs about, emotional reactions to, and treatment of others often seem small to us (as we are single drops of rain), but we often do not know the downpour of droplets others might be experiencing—especially if we have different lived experiences than they do.

To better understand whether discrimination might be hidden somewhere in your organization, review what metrics might be available. For example, do people with different identities get paid the same amount of money for doing the same job? Pay inequity is common in many organizations, with women and racial minorities getting paid less for the same work. You might also want to explore whether people from different identity groups are more likely to apply for positions or are more likely to be offered similar roles, promotions, and challenging assignments. It is also important to compare credentials. Do different groups of people tend to have higher credentials or more experience and yet get offered the same roles or salary as other people? Who gets hired or promoted based on experience, and who gets hired or promoted based on potential?

If your organization does not currently track any of these metrics, working with people analytics or an HR specialist to set up such metrics is also a good place to start.

ORGANIZATIONAL APPROACHES TO DECREASING STEREOTYPES, PREJUDICE, AND DISCRIMINATION

Organizations that want to remain competitive in today's marketplace need to be equitable, diverse, and inclusive—both in order to attract and attain talent, and to improve innovation and revenue. There is significant evidence that diverse groups outperform non-diverse when it comes to problem solving and innovation.[12] Additional findings show that intentionally diverse and inclusive groups are more productive, have better employee engagement, and even perform better financially.[13][14]

To successfully recruit, support, retain, and activate a diverse workgroup, it is vital to not only gain an awareness of the types of diversity within and across groups, but to understand the inherent complications of having individuals from a wide range of backgrounds and perspectives work together. A major challenge that comes with diverse groups is the possibility of increased stereotypes, discrimination, and prejudice.[15][16] This is especially likely when a group's diversity changes drastically, or in the case of extreme diverse viewpoints that cannot be reconciled, leading to break downs in communication and alignment.

Contemporary researchers and organizational experts have spent a lot of effort trying to determine how to best create and support diverse workplaces that limit stereotypes, prejudice, and discrimination. Initially, some suggested a "colorblind" or "difference-blind" ideology. These approaches support the idea that everyone should be treated equally, and de-emphasizes and downplays differences in social identity. At first, this idea

REFLECTION

Does your organization take a "colorblind" approach or a "diversity-focused" approach to identity and difference? What evidence do you have of this? What initiatives might you want to consider now that you know more about these two types of approaches?

makes intuitive sense. After all, if all of these differences around in-groups and out-groups are causing harm and disruption, downplaying or ignoring such differences seems wise. However, research found that these approaches backfired. In fact, colorblind approaches to workplace diversity actually increased bias and decreased accountability of discrimination compared to diversity-focused ideologies[17][18]. Psychologists believe that this is because social identity categorizations happen somewhat automatically; therefore, we may not be truly capable of social identity "blindness." Instead, a colorblind stance limits our ability to recognize and address discrimination, leading to minority groups feeling even more marginalized because it communicates that what has been a lived experience for them doesn't exist in the eyes of others.[19]

Abby Ferber, the director of the Matrix Center for the Advancement of Social Equality and Inclusion, states that while "blind" ideologies are theoretically meant to promote equal treatment, in reality, they mask privilege. When social identity differences are ignored, the majority is seen as "normal"—rather than privileged—and, consequently, minorities who speak up are blamed for 'choosing to focus on differences'.[20] In this situation, diversity is not being effectively leveraged and supported; rather, it is being tamped down and ignored as employees are told to be "blind" to difference.

Instead, "multicultural" or "diversity-focused" approaches in the workplace seem to be more effective.[21] These approaches emphasize the idea that diversity and differences should be recognized, respected, and celebrated. Examples of diversity-focused approaches include initiatives such as employee resource groups (ERGs) for different social identities (e.g., a group for women or LGBTQA employees). These groups allow individuals from similar backgrounds across an organization to connect and support each other. Other diversity-focused initiatives might include holidays or celebrations that recognize different groups' traditions and cultures or efforts made to increase representations of various social identity groups at different levels of the organization.

3

Challenging the Habit of Bias: The SCRIPt™ Toolkit

Recognizing, challenging, and dismantling bias (and more specifically, stereotypes, prejudice, and discrimination) is a central part of promoting justice, equity, diversity, and inclusion in the workplace and the world. However, it is easy to feel overwhelmed and confused about how to best address these issues. In this section of the book, we will share strategies research has demonstrated to be effective in mitigating bias. These practices are Self-care, Contact, Recognize & Replace, Information, and Perspective taking. These techniques will help you recognize your own bias, better notice when bias happens around you, and begin breaking bias habits. An easy way to remember these practices is with the acronym SCRIPt™. We refer to these practices as the SCRIPt™ toolkit.

OTHER STUDIES HAVE SHOWN THAT
MINDFULNESS, MEDITATION, OR OTHER
PRACTICES THAT MAKE YOU FEEL CALM,
FOCUSED, AND CENTERED CAN LOWER YOUR
PERSONAL BIAS LEVELS. MINDFULNESS IS
ABOUT INTENTIONALLY FOCUSING ON THE
PRESENT MOMENT, WITHOUT JUDGMENT.

SELF-CARE

You may be surprised to learn that one of the best ways to decrease your bias is to tend to your own well-being. Research has consistently shown that we are more likely to slip into biased thoughts, emotions, and behaviors when we are tired, stressed, or distracted. For example, a study published in *Nature* found that people running on four hours of sleep had increased negative implicit associations towards Arab Muslims compared to when the same individuals were well-rested.[22] Another study found that chronically sleep-deprived people were more likely to rate pictures of out-group races as "dangerous."[23] So, a simple good night's sleep has the power to modify both implicit bias and explicit decisions and evaluations of others.

Sleep increases your self-awareness, emotion regulation, decision-making, and concentration—skills needed for effective leadership and to prevent bias. Yet, rest is often among the first things we sacrifice because of personal and professional time demands. It's recommended that the average person should sleep for seven to nine hours, but a recent CCL research study reports that 42% of leaders get only six or fewer hours of sleep a night.[24]

Other studies have shown that mindfulness, meditation, or other practices that make you feel calm, focused, and centered can lower your personal bias levels. Mindfulness is about intentionally focusing on the present moment, without judgment. A common method for inducing mindfulness is to meditate or to focus on your breathing. However, mindfulness can be induced by simply focusing on any part of your experience of the present moment, such as what you are seeing, feeling, smelling, or hearing. Mindfulness brings a sense of presence, neutrality, and of being grounded. This clarity is instrumental in recognizing biases and breaking your bias habits. For example, one study found that listening to a 10-minute mindfulness audio guide decreased negative implicit associations related to race and age.[25] Mindfulness has also been shown to increase trust and decrease discrimination and in-group bias in tasks that require cooperation among team members, as well as decrease correspondence bias.[26] [27]

Self-care can feel self-indulgent or superficial, but when it comes to leadership, self-care is about making sure you are showing up at your best for the sake of leading others. Think of self-care like the safety demonstration on a flight: if you don't put on your own mask first, you will not be able to help others with their masks.

Take action: There are many ways to practice self-care. Anything that lets you approach your work and your team refreshed, focused, calm, and curious will help mitigate bias. To get you started, here are some tips and approaches for practicing self-care.

- **Prioritize sleep.** Getting enough sleep will decrease the chances that you will slip into biased responses due to an exhausted brain. To make sure you're getting enough sleep, try:

  » Keeping bedtimes and wake-times consistent. By minimizing variation in your sleep schedule, you're less likely to confuse your body and make it harder to fall asleep and/or wake up.

» Getting 20 more minutes. If you're feeling tired or like you did not get enough sleep, consider finding a place in your schedule to add 20 minutes of sleep. It can be 20 extra minutes before waking up, a 20-minute nap in the middle of the day, or going to bed 20 minutes earlier than usual.

» Minimizing blue light before you go to sleep. To prevent blue light from interfering with sleep, turn off devices at least one hour before bed or consider using a blue light filter (e.g., "night mode" on a smartphone).

- **Clock Out.** The modern conveniences of technology and remote work means that many of us can work anywhere at anytime. Unfortunately, this also means that many leaders feel like they are always on the clock and unable to psychologically detach from work—which leads to burn out, stress, and difficulty sleeping. Self care involves setting work life boundaries. For example, not working after a certain time of day, or not bringing work with you on vacation or family events. Determine what boundaries work best for your life and then stick to it.

- **Just Breathe.** Many mindfulness and meditation interventions center on teaching people how to use their breath as an anchor—a grounding force you can always rely on. Your breath is always present (keeping you focused on the here and now rather than the past or future), and always with you, no matter where you are. Consider taking a few moments to learn a simple yet effective breathing exercise so that you can use it in moments of stress. For example, one simple exercise is to breathe in for a count of four and breathe out for a count of six.

- **Connect to Your Senses.** Like your breath, your five senses (taste, touch, smell, sight, hearing) offers you ways to connect to the present moment. Doing so can help you disconnect from stress and thought spirals which are likely to escalate bias. Practice doing a "sense check" when you need to clear your mind: pick a sense and engage with an activity that fully immerses that sense. For example, you can listen to a favorite song to engage your sense of hearing or focus on the smell of a particular flower (e.g., a peony) by smelling it over and over again.

CONTACT

Another simple way to decrease bias is by increasing contact with people from different backgrounds and lived experiences. We tend to gravitate towards others who are similar to us, but this gravitation often reinforces in-group, affinity, and confirmation bias. After all, it's much easier to hold stereotypes and prejudices towards groups or individuals you do not interact with very often.

Research shows that exposure to diverse groups of people is an effective way to decrease bias. For example, living in highly multiracial environments and/or having more racially diverse friends results in lower levels of racial stereotypes, racial ingroup bias, and race-related anxiety.[28] Similar effects have also been found when examining interactions with people who differ in terms of national origin, philosophies of life, and political or religious beliefs.[29]

It is worth noting that initial contact with new groups may stir feelings of fear, anxiety, or discomfort. Simply acknowledging your emotions and not getting caught up in them can keep such emotions from taking over. The more frequently you engage with others who are different from you, share positive experiences with them, and keep an open mind, the more you replace your prior thoughts and feelings with new associations.

Take action: How much contact do you have with different groups of people in your life? Are most of your friends fairly similar? Or are they diverse? What about the people with whom you work? Reflect on whether you have enough contact with different groups and whether there are opportunities for change. Here are a few examples of how you could consider increasing contact in your life and your organization.

- **Increase your contact through media.** When it comes to media, do you tend to pay attention to specific groups? How could you expand who you hear from?

  For example, if you have a Twitter account, review who you follow. If you notice you mostly follow a specific gender, race, viewpoint, etc., consider who you could add to expand the voices you hear from.

  Similarly, consider whether you tend to read about or watch documentaries that focus on a specific perspective or experience. Consider what you might do to expand your exposure to different stories.

- **Consider contact when assigning projects.** Next time you put together a project or initiative, actively consider who you are including. Is everyone on the team from the same department? From the same office? From the same gender, race, or generation? How can you add diversity to a team and thereby encourage contact across groups?

- **Celebrate diversity.** At the organization level, consider hosting or sponsoring cultural events or bringing in speakers who can share insights relevant to different identities. This is a great way to increase contact and awareness across the organization.

- **Design spaces with contact in mind.** Contact can play a role in workplace design. How is your physical workplace organized? Are there opportunities for people from different backgrounds to cross paths? Or are people segregated (by department, leader level, generation, race, or gender)? What can you do, or what can you change, to increase contact across backgrounds?

RECOGNIZE & REPLACE

Research indicates that simply ignoring or not thinking about bias is not an effective approach to changing bias habits. In fact, some research has found that simply trying to 'suppress' stereotypes (e.g., actively trying not to think about them) can have a backlash effect and make bias even worse.[30] Because of this, it's important you not just recognize bias but replace your initial reactions with non-biased ones.

Recognize & replace is a multi-step strategy to change your bias habits. It requires you first to recognize a biased or stereotypical response and then consider how to replace it to break down your previous associations to prevent stereotypes, prejudice and discrimination. This strategy is particularly effective for addressing stereotypes, as it is a thought exercise, and stereotypes often reside in our thoughts. For example, if you find yourself hesitating over a job applicant's resume, thinking, **But what if their English isn't good?** or **But what if they are lazy?** consider whether a stereotype is at the root of your thought. If you recognize that the thought was rooted in a stereotype, acknowledge this and replace the reaction with a non-stereotypical one. For example, think of someone you know with a similar background who speaks perfect English. Or imagine this job applicant showing up and being the opposite of these stereotypes. Research has shown that recognize & replace is a useful thought exercise that can help you break the habit of bias over time.[31]

Recognize & replace can also be used as a way to make changes in your organization. For example, research suggests that there is a stereotype that associates men with being more likely to be seen as "brilliant" and "geniuses." Because of this, men are more likely to get "perfect 10s" on a 1 to 10 performance review systems in the workplace. However, some evaluators recognized this and replaced the scoring system with a scale from 1 to 6. Because "6" is not associated with perfect, they reasoned that this scale would be less biased; and indeed, they found that when evaluation ratings were on this scale, the gender differences disappeared.[32]

Take action: Here are some ways you can start recognizing and replacing bias in your life.

- **Pay attention to stereotypical representations** in your thoughts, actions, or surroundings. Bias is difficult to detect unless you're attending to it. With practice, it becomes more obvious. For example, try paying attention to stereotypical representations in TV shows or commercials or the images used in your organization's promotional materials.

- **Ask yourself hard questions.** If you notice yourself thinking, feeling, or acting on something that may be rooted in bias, ask yourself, "Does the thought I'm having reflect a stereotype?" or "Is this response biased?" If you answer "yes," acknowledge it as such. This may be painful to do; no one likes admitting that they have made an assumption about someone. You may rationalize that you didn't mean to stereotype or that you had good reason, in this case, to do so. But like any habit you're trying to break, your first step is acknowledging the issue. Recognizing and labeling stereotypes are critical initial steps in combating bias.

- **Acknowledge the consequences.** Once you've noticed a stereotype or bias—in your head or out in the world—spend a few moments exploring the potential consequences of the stereotype: "What does this make me want to do?" or "What could be the consequences of putting this belief into action?" Acknowledge these possibilities.

- **Replace what you've recognized.** Finally, with the insight gained from your reflection, consider a different, unbiased response that you could substitute in its place, such as creating a detailed, non-stereotypical image in your mind. Or recalling evidence—even anecdotal—that disputes the

stereotype. Or, if you have the power, do something to
replace the stereotypical representation out in the world.

INFORMATION

Your brain is designed to offer shortcuts and best guesses
whenever possible to minimize the cognitive effort it takes you to
process your environment. Unfortunately, such shortcuts often rely
on assumptions, stereotypes and implicit associations. Information
is a strategy you can use to counteract your brain's autopilot and
become better at noticing bias.

Information is about asking questions, gathering data, and
challenging assumptions. For example, women are less likely to get
international assignments, partly because managers worry about
putting women in such positions. There are often concerns that
women will feel uncomfortable relocating, have a more challenging
time balancing family obligations, or have difficulty adjusting to
gender roles abroad. These well-intended, protective hesitations
are unsupported by empirical evidence, which largely shows that
women are interested in international assignments and perform
them well.[33] Moreover, international experience is often seen
as a necessary experience for moving up the leadership ladder.
Therefore, well-meaning leaders who try to protect women from
potentially tough or unpleasant experiences end up, ironically,
holding them back.

A focus on information gathering can help you avoid such traps.
By exploring metrics and research, and simply asking questions
over making assumptions, you decrease the chances of making a
well-intentioned protective hesitation that could backfire.

Take action: Here are productive steps you can take to seek information:

- **Look for what's missing.** Consider what information you have and what you don't know for sure. Incomplete information may lead you to false assumptions and biased conclusions. Assessing what you don't know may reveal an information gap and help direct your search for additional information.

- **Ask questions first.** When you're faced with making decisions that impact others, ask clarifying questions, and seek others' input before proceeding.

- **Do your research.** If you are facing a specific challenge or issue, find reliable sources to inform your decision. Many scholarly articles and subject matter experts can help you make sure you're not inadvertently perpetuating bias.

- **Gather data.** One of the most powerful ways to reveal—and address—bias, stereotypes, prejudice, and discrimination in the workplace is to gather data. Numbers, figures, and feedback can reveal if there is a disparity in opportunities or unequal treatment, such as gender differences in pay or race differences in promotion.

PERSPECTIVE TAKING

Perspective taking consists of adopting the viewpoint of someone different from you and imagining yourself living with their perspective. Science has shown that stepping outside your own experience to view things from another person's perspective is an effective way to decrease bias. For example, one Harvard study conducted with the U.S. Army found that soldiers who completed perspective-taking training were more accurate at detecting bias in others—including in-group bias, confirmation bias, and correspondence bias.[34] They were also better able to develop a rationale for others' behaviors and adapt their logic when faced with new evidence.

Another study found that when people were instructed to take the perspective of someone from a different race, their automatic negative associations and self-reported feelings of prejudice towards that race decreased.[35] But, even more importantly and impressively, when those same people were later asked to interact with someone from the race they were perspective taking, the other-race person rated their interactions more positively than those who did not first practice perspective taking.

Perspective taking also increases your ability to detect—and accurately assess—inequity and discrimination around you. For example, a study found that perspective taking increased people's ability to notice discrimination within an institutional sexism case—but only if legitimate evidence of discrimination was presented.[36] In other words, perspective taking resulted in a more accurate assessment of the situation: it did not simply bias results in the other direction.

Take action: Some ways you can practice perspective taking include:

- **Imagine a day in the life.** Think of someone from a different background or perspective than you. It could be a coworker, a spouse, a supervisor, or even a fictional character or celebrity.

Imagine a day in this individual's life as if you were that person, seeing the world through their eyes and walking through the world in their shoes.

- **Write a journal entry as someone else.** If you are having a hard time understanding a colleague's point of view on a project or decision, try writing a journal entry "as they might" by writing a first-person narrative from their perspective of what happened in the given situation. When you write as the other person, things may appear different to you.

- **Practice active listening.** You can also improve your perspective taking by using active listening when you interact with others. When someone comes to you with a problem or issue, or even just to share a recent experience, give all of your attention to them. Turn off your cell phone and put away your work. Listen to what the speaker is saying, rather than thinking about your own needs or what you plan to say next. Pay attention to the feelings and values expressed by the speaker's tone of voice and their body language. Non-verbal messages can often reveal more than words. If anything is unclear, ask follow-up questions to ensure you understand thoroughly. Imagine as best you can what it must be like to be in your speaker's situation.

- **Pause and take some perspective.** When you notice yourself having a negative reaction to someone else, stop and take a moment to take the perspective of that person. Consider asking yourself the following questions: *What might I be feeling, thinking, feeling? How would I feel if I knew another person had thought this about me? What*

kinds of things may be affecting me that I don't tell other people? Such simple questions can help reveal a different perspective to a situation and prevent your mind from jumping to conclusions or making assumptions that might be based on biases.

While this section describes "SCRIPt™" as five separate tools, in practice, there is some overlap between them. In any given situation, you might find yourself using one or multiple tools, or finding that you address multiple aspects of SCRIPt™ within the same response. This is perfectly natural, as the tools all help support and reinforce each other—offering different angles and prompts for approaching the same issues. For example, in an effort to effectively perspective-take, you may find yourself asking questions and trying to gather information (tapping into the "information" tool) and/or actively seeking out perspectives from people different from yourself (tapping into the "contact" tool) to better understand diverse viewpoints. Do not worry too much about trying to identify whether a behavior is one tool or the other. Rather, use the SCRIPt™ acronym to help you come up with ideas and options for addressing bias in your own life. The next section offers some examples of how you can use the SCRIPt™ toolkit and personalize it to your specific circumstances and challenges.

SCRIPt™ IN ACTION

As with any useful toolkit, SCRIPt™ offers you various options that can help you build something new. But of course, tools are only helpful if you use them. You don't need to use every tool every time, and it is up to you to determine what tools are appropriate for a given situation. We recommend that you spend some time reflecting on which SCRIPt™ tools might assist you in your specific situation in work and life. It will probably help if you start by thinking of one aspect or issue related to bias you would like to address. To give you some inspiration for what SCRIPt™ can look like in action, here are three examples of three different leaders using SCRIPt™ to navigate and decrease bias at work.

EXAMPLE 1: NICO IN HR

As an HR leader, Nico oversees recruiting new talent for his organization. After going through his Beyond Bias book, he decides to use SCRIPt™ to examine any potential bias in hiring in his organization. Starting with Information, he looks through his HR information system and realizes his organization has collected very little data regarding the social identities of people who apply for jobs. Without this information, it's hard to know what biases might be present in the company's hiring practices. Nico starts to think through questions to help reveal relevant opportunities when it comes to this particular issue. How might he gather information to discover whether they are getting a diverse group of applicants? Are there any social identities missing from their applicant pool? If so, why?

Nico also realizes he needs to gather information on the diversity of new hires and applicants to see whether there is a gap between the diversity of people applying and the diversity of people being hired. Nico creates a process for asking applicants to answer questions about their social identities as part of an equity, diversity, and inclusion initiative. He also starts tracking information about how applicants hear about a position, who gets hired, and who declines a job.

Six months later, the data is in. Nico discovers that the application pool is not as diverse as he would have guessed. A few social identity groups seem well represented, but the rest are not. In fact, a couple of social identity groups seem absent altogether. He also realizes that a strikingly high number of applicants heard about the job from a friend. Given that people often naturally gravitate towards others like themselves—and that increasing diversity requires increasing contact—Nico decides that relying on word of mouth might be limiting their application pool. He invests in advertising future job descriptions more widely and does some research on who is likely to see ads posted in different sources to make sure his readership is as broad as possible.

As he reviews the job description materials, Nico also starts to wonder whether there are any unintentional associations between the terms he uses to describe the job and certain cultural or gender identities. He runs the job description through a free online tool to analyze whether his words are biased and is surprised to find several words are flagged as highly "masculine." Nico remembers the "R" in SCRIPt™: it is not enough to recognize biases; they have to be replaced. He works with his team to reword the job description with more neutral words.

Three months later, when he looks back at his metrics, Nico sees a broader group of individuals applying for positions.

Because he also tracked who is getting hired, he also sees that the demographic breakdown of those who get hired matches the initial application pool. This suggests that there seems to be little bias in who gets hired, and the primary bias issue was around who applied to work at the organization.

EXAMPLE 2: AVERY IN MIDDLE MANAGEMENT

Avery is a mid-level manager that leads several teams. After reading the Beyond Bias book, she wants to take a more in-depth look into how bias might affect her ability to lead.

In the past, Avery thought that constant stress and busyness was a normal part of her job. But now, knowing that stress could

REFLECTION

What is one specific bias-related issue you would like to tackle in your work or life? It could be related to a specific social group (e.g., support for Black women engineers, positive experiences for international students, resources for neuro-atypical readers, etc.). Or it could be related to a specific process or issue in your organization (e.g., how people are hired, who gets invited to board meetings, what words are used in written materials). It could even be unrelated to the workplace (e.g., what identities are represented in your child's media consumption or education). Be as specific as possible. Why are you motivated to address this issue? What can you do about it, given your sphere of influence? What is one step you can take to explore this issue? Who can help you with this challenge?

be harming others by distorting her personal bias, she can't ignore it any longer. Of course, Avery doesn't magically become less stressed. However, she does start thinking about her self-care practices regarding big events and decisions that impact other people. For instance, since Avery feels most rested and focused in the mornings, she commits to review employee hiring, promotion, and performance materials at the start of the day. In the past, she often put off such paperwork until the end of the day, even reviewing materials in bed—a practice she now realizes could have led her exhausted brain to rely on shortcuts and assumptions, distorting her evaluations and perhaps negatively impacting others' careers.

She also starts taking days off when she needs them to keep her from getting burned out and goes for a run on tough days (her favorite way to burn off stress). She also takes up a new habit of meditating for a few minutes before meetings with her team to help her be present. While she still works hard for her team, Avery knows that if she is not in a good place mentally, physically, and emotionally, her team will likely be the ones who suffer.

Avery also realizes that she has little information about whether her team has ever experienced her actions as discriminatory or biased. She gets the courage to do a 360-degree assessment, asking her employees and colleagues to share their feedback anonymously. To her immense relief, the results are mostly positive, even complimentary. However, she does discover that others were seeing patterns in her behavior she wasn't aware of. For instance, some of her younger employees felt she didn't take them seriously because of their age and was condescending towards them. Avery was shocked to hear this, as she had thought of herself as being an excellent mentor. However, she knows that one of the challenges with bias is that well-intentioned actions can often still have a negative impact on others.

Now that Avery has recognized this issue, she works on replacing it. Any time she notices she might be talking down to her younger employees, she commits to pausing, taking a breath, and asking them for their advice, expertise, or perspective. Avery hopes that this perspective taking will help her employees see that she values their opinions, allowing her to learn more about how they are experiencing a given situation.

Through these steps, Avery's relationships with her employees improve, and Avery feels more confident that she is treating people fairly and with respect.

EXAMPLE 3: ROWAN IN MARKETING

Rowan is a web designer and copy editor in marketing. After reading this book, the bias challenge they want to tackle is to improve how different social identity groups are represented visually on their company's website. The first thing they notice is that there appears to be some stereotypical representation when it comes to gender: most "boss" images are of men, while women seem to be visually represented as assistants, secretaries, and caregivers. Rowan remembers the "R" in SCRIPt™ and is pleased they were able to recognize and label these stereotypes. There also seems to be little diversity in what types of women and men are represented—everyone seems to be of about the same age and body type, and all are dressed traditionally and conservatively. Looking at the images with this lens, Rowan is able to replace some images with new images that represent a broader spectrum of gender roles and expressions to make the website more gender-inclusive.

However, as Rowan continues to look through their materials, they notice that other social identity groups, such as religion, sexual orientation, and (dis)ability, do not seem to be visually represented at all. Rowan is surprised by this realization. At the same time, they are not sure how to be inclusive of these groups since they know that these social identities can sometimes be invisible. Unsure what to do about this, they think through their SCRIPt™ toolkit and decide to do some perspective taking: What would it be like to come to a website that did not have their social identities represented? Rowan decides it wouldn't feel great, but also thinks it would be even worse to have these social identities poorly represented. They imagine going to a website that only had a stereotypical representation of an identity that was central to who they are and how insulting that would be. They also imagined how excited they would be to view a website that did right by their social identity groups.

Knowing that representation is both sensitive and important, they decide they don't have enough information or regular contact with the social identity groups in question to represent them appropriately or make these decisions alone. Instead, Rowan sets up meetings with their organization's employee resource groups for these social identities, shares their vision, and asks for input. Rowan learns a lot, and they mock up some ideas for how to be more visually inclusive. Finally, they present their changes to both their manager and an external focus group. Both groups give Rowan some additional suggestions, but overall they are impressed with how much more inclusive the website looks with these small changes, and all agree that the changes will improve the company's brand.

CONCLUSION

Bias is pervasive and harmful, and yet often unintentional. If left unchecked in the workplace, bias can decrease the effectiveness of individual leaders, limit the career trajectories of certain social identity groups, and even damage the culture of entire organizations. This book can help you tackle bias in the workplace by 1) increasing your understanding of bias, what it looks like, and how it is linked to social identities, stereotypes, discrimination and prejudice; 2) giving you practical and actionable ideas for what you can do to decrease your personal bias as well as decrease bias in your organization.

Addressing bias requires you to practice self-care, broaden your engagement with diverse groups, replace biased and stereotypical responses, focus on gathering information, and consider other's perspectives. By consistently and persistently working through the reflections and actions in this book, you can break down the habit of bias and increase justice, equity, diversity, and inclusion in the workplace and in your life.

BIBLIOGRAPHY

1   Begley, S. (2006). He, once a she, offers own view on science spat. *The Wall Street Journal*. https://www.wsj.com/articles/SB115274744775305134

2   MacMillan Dictionary. Origin of the word bias. Retrieved from: https://www.macmillandictionaryblog.com/bias

3   Greenwald, A. G., & Krieger, L. H. (2006). Implicit bias: Scientific foundations. *California Law Review*, 94(4), 945-967. http://faculty.washington.edu/agg/pdf/Gwald%26Krieger.CLR.2006.pdf

4   Chambers, D. W. (1983). Stereotypic images of the scientist: The draw-a-scientist test. *Science Education*, 67(2), 255-265.

5   Andrews, B. R. (1903). Habit. *The American Journal of Psychology*, 14(2), 121-149.

6   Jerald, M. C., Cole, E. R., Ward, L. M., & Avery, L. R. (2017). Controlling images: How awareness of group stereotypes affects Black women's well-being. *Journal of Counseling Psychology*, 64(5), 487.

7   Shih, M., Pittinsky, T. L., & Ambady, N. (1999). Stereotype susceptibility: Identity salience and shifts in quantitative performance. *Psychological Science*, 10(1), 80-83.

8   Dovidio, John F., John C. Brigham, Blair T. Johnson, and Samuel L. Gaertner. "Stereotyping, prejudice, and discrimination: Another look." *Stereotypes and Stereotyping*, 276 (1996): 319.

9   Fiske, S. T. (1998). Stereotyping, prejudice, and discrimination. *The Handbook of Social Psychology*, 2(4), 357-411.

10 Fekedulegn, D., Alterman, T., Charles, L. E., Kershaw, K. N., Safford, M. M., Howard, V. J., & MacDonald, L. A. (2019). Prevalence of workplace discrimination and mistreatment in a national sample of older US workers: The REGARDS cohort study. *SSM—Population Health*, 8, 100444.

11 Pager, D., & Western, B. (2012). Identifying discrimination at work: The use of field experiments. *Journal of Social*

Issues, 68(2), 221-237.

12   Dreifus, C. (2008). In professor's model, diversity = productivity. The New York Times. https://www.nytimes.com/2008/01/08/science/08conv.html

13   Page, Scott. (2007). *The Difference: How the Power of Diversity Creates Better Groups, Firms, Schools, and Societies* (New Edition).

14   Schaufeli W. B., Martinez I. M., Marques-Pinto A., Salanova M., Bakker A. B. (2002a). Burnout and engagement in university students: a cross-national study. *Journal of Cross-Cultural Psychology*. 33, 464–481. 10.1177/0022022102033005003

15   Hurtado, S., Carter, D. F. and Kardia, D. (1998). The climate for diversity: Key issues for institutional self-study. *New Directions for Institutional Research*, 1998: 53–63. doi: 10.1002/ir.9804

16   Plant & Devine (2003). The antecedents and implications of interracial anxiety. *Personality and Social Psychology Bulletin*, 29(6), 790-801.

17   Richeson, J. A., & Nussbaum, R. J. (2004). The impact of multiculturalism versus color-blindness on racial bias. *Journal of Experimental Social Psychology*, 40, 417–423.

18   Wolsko, C., Park, B., Judd, C. M., & Wittenbrink, B. (2000). Framing interethnic ideology: Effects of multicultural and color-blind perspectives on judgments of groups and individuals. *Journal of Personality and Social Psychology*, 78, 635–654.

19   Plaut, V., Thomas, K. M. & Goren, M. J. (2009). Is multiculturalism or colorblindness better for minorities? *Psychological Science*, 20(4).

20   Ferber, A. L., (2012) The culture of privilege: Color-blindess, postfeminism, and christonormativity. *Journal of Social Issues*, 68(1), p.63-77.

21   Wolsko, C., Park, B., Judd, C. M., & Wittenbrink, B. (2000). Framing interethnic ideology: Effects of multicultural and color-blind perspectives on judgments of groups and individuals. *Journal of Personality and Social Psychology*, 78, 635–654.

22   Alkozei, A., Killgore, W. D., Smith, R., Dailey, N. S., Bajaj, S., & Haack, M. (2017). Chronic sleep restriction increases negative implicit attitudes toward Arab Muslims. *Scientific Reports*, 7(1), 1-6. https://www.nature.com/articles/s41598-017-04585-w

23   Alkozei, A., Haack, M., Skalamera, J., Smith, R., Satterfield, B. C., Raikes, A. C., & Killgore, W. D. (2018). Chronic sleep restriction affects the association between implicit bias and explicit social decision making. *Sleep Health*, 4(5), 456-462.

24   Clerkin, C., Ruderman, M. N., & Svetieva, E. (2017). *Tired at work: A roadblock to effective leadership* (White paper). Center for Creative Leadership, Greensboro, NC.

25   Lueke, A., & Gibson, B. (2015). Mindfulness meditation reduces implicit age and race bias: The role of reduced automaticity of responding. *Social Psychological and Personality Science*, 6(3), 284-291.

26   Lueke, A., & Gibson, B. (2016). Brief mindfulness meditation reduces discrimination. *Psychology of Consciousness: Theory, Research, and Practice*, 3(1), 34.

27   Hopthrow, T., Hooper, N., Mahmood, L., Meier, B.P. & Weger, U. (2017). Mindfulness reduces the correspondence bias. *The Quarterly Journal of Experimental Psychology*, 70(3), pp. 351-360. doi: 10.1080/17470218.2016.1149498

28   Pauker, K., Carpinella, C., Meyers, C., Young, D. M., & Sanchez, D. T. (2018). The role of diversity exposure in Whites' reduction in race essentialism over time. *Social Psychological and Personality Science*, 9(8), 944-952.

29   Holoien, D. S. (2013). *Do differences make a difference. The effects of diversity on learning, intergroup outcomes, and civic engagement*. Princeton, NJ: Princeton University.

30   Galinsky, A. D., & Moskowitz, G. B. (2000). Perspective-taking: decreasing stereotype expression, stereotype accessibility, and in-group favoritism. *Journal of Personality and Social Psychology*, 78(4), 708.

31   Devine, P. G., Forscher, P. S., Cox, W. T., Kaatz, A., Sheridan, J., & Carnes, M. (2017). A gender bias habit-breaking intervention led to increased hiring of female faculty in STEMM departments. *Journal of Experimental Social Psychology*, 73, 211-215.

32   Rivera, L., and Tilscik, A. (2019). One way to reduce gender bias in performance reviews. Harvard Business Review. https://hbr.org/2019/04/one-way-to-reduce-gender-bias-in-performance-reviews

33   Clerkin, C., & Wilson, M. S. (2017). Gender differences in developmental experiences. *In Handbook of research on gender and leadership*. Edward Elgar Publishing.

34   Gehlbach, H., Young, L. V., & Roan, L. K. (2012). Teaching social perspective taking: How educators might learn from the Army. *Educational Psychology*, 32(3), 295-309.

35   Todd, A. R., Bodenhausen, G. V., Richeson, J. A., & Galinsky, A. D. (2011). Perspective taking combats automatic expressions of racial bias. *Journal of Personality and Social Psychology*, 100(6), 1027.

36   Simon, S., Magaldi, M. E., & O'Brien, L. T. (2019). Empathy versus evidence: Does perspective-taking for a discrimination claimant bias judgments of institutional sexism? *Group Processes & Intergroup Relations*, 22(8), 1109-1123.

ABOUT THE CENTER FOR CREATIVE LEADERSHIP

The Center for Creative Leadership (CCL©) is a top-ranked, global provider of leadership development. By leveraging the power of leadership to drive results that matter most to clients, CCL transforms individual leaders, teams, organizations, and society. Our array of cutting-edge solutions is steeped in extensive research and experience gained from working with hundreds of thousands of leaders at all levels. Ranked among the world's top providers of executive education, CCL has offices in countries worldwide.

CPSIA information can be obtained
at www.ICGtesting.com
Printed in the USA
BVHW061352030222
627505BV00003B/6